Boxed Out

Boxed Out

7 Steps to a Spiritually Productive Life

ROBIN SMOOT

Copyright © 2016 by Robin Smoot. All rights reserved.

No portion of this book may be reproduced or transmitted in any form or by any means, electronic or mechanical, including photocopying and recording, or by any information storage and retrieval system, without permission in writing from the publisher.

Published by Robin Smoot, P. O. Box 324, Knightdale, NC 27545
www.LiveBoxedOut.com

ISBN 978-0692665831

Editing by LifeSlice Media

All Scripture quotations are taken from The Holy Bible, New International Version, unless otherwise indicated.

Printed in the United States of America

DISCLAIMER: This book details the author's personal experiences with and opinions about being an entrepreneur. The author is not licensed as a counsellor, teacher, psychologist, or psychiatrist. Neither the author or publisher, nor any authors, contributors, or other representatives will be liable for damages arising out of or in connection with the use of this book. This is a comprehensive limitation of liability that applies to all damages of any kind, including (without limitation) compensatory; direct, indirect or consequential damages; loss of data, income or profit; loss of or damage to property and claims of third parties. You understand that this book is not intended as a substitute for consultation with a licensed medical, educational, legal or psychiatric professional. Before you begin any change in your lifestyle in any way, you will consult a licensed professional to ensure that you are doing what's best for your situation. This book provides content related to educational or motivational topics. As such, use of this book implies your acceptance of this disclaimer.

To Kevin, Rhyan, and Bryson.
May you always see the world through God lenses.

Acknowledgements

God, my Father, Savior, Master, and Friend, I thank you for loving me and choosing me before I was born. You have saved my life from things known and unknown so that I could live for you. Thank you for your grace and mercy that supersede my faults and imperfections. It is because of you alone that this assignment is complete, and I trust you to work it into your master plan. I pray that you bless each reader; cause them to draw closer to you and show them what your perfect will is for their lives.

My husband, Kevin. Thank you for always seeing and supporting my endeavors. Through times of plenty and times when we didn't have a dime of our own, you always encouraged me to follow God's lead. I follow His as I follow you. Thank you for listening to my mind dumps, letting me act goofy, and not complaining that I didn't have time for you as I completed this assignment. I have and will always love you, and I am blessed by your presence in my life.

My precious children – Kevin, Rhyan, and Bryson. You inspire me each day by your creativity, your heart for others, and your love of Jesus. Thank you for your patience as I spent hours in my office and away from you. I love you more than I could ever write or say.

My grandma, Gussie Wallace, I don't know if you'll see these words in heaven, but you have to know that I love and miss you beyond words. Thank you for demonstrating Christ in all seasons. I can't wait to see you again. To my mom, Laura Wallace, and my aunts Gloria & Sabrina, your daily demonstration of faith - especially during difficult times – inspires me more than you know. I love you dearly.

My sista-girl, Priscilla Woodson, your hustle for the Lord is unlike anything I've ever seen. We've been journeying together for years, and we ain't done yet!

Finally, to all of my family, friends, and clients, I am truly thankful for each of you, and I pray for your continued forward movement.

Contents

Acknowledgements	vii
Living Boxed Out	11
1 - Believe Bigger	21
2 - Accept Your Assignment	27
3 - Demolish Your Walls	37
4 - Take Inventory	57
5 - Plan For Success	65
6 - Work It Out	79
7 - Chase The Horizon	93
Epilogue	105
References	106
About The Author	107

Living Boxed Out

This book is not about basketball. Yes, I understand that the phrase "boxing out" is often used to coach players to be better rebounders. And while I do enjoy watching a good game every now and then, I can assure you that there is absolutely no way I will ever be qualified to give you any athletic instruction. None whatsoever.

So let's just set the record straight right now: Boxing out in the sense you'll discover in the following seven chapters is not about defense. In fact, it's more about offense. You will learn how to trust in your Coach, follow His plan and carry out His plays. You will learn how to draw on the fundamentals and use your unique skills to crush the opposition. You will discover that you are a starter in this game and you will never sit on the bench. When you get fouled, you'll take one for the team and keep on playing. And you'll do all of this in an arena of onlookers who will want to know how you came to play so well and why you seem to enjoy it so much. You will "get buckets" as you convert skeptics to followers, and ultimately, you will emerge victorious. But I did say this wasn't about basketball, didn't I?

The concept for this book came to me after another unfulfilling, frustrating day on the job - much like any other day that I've had to go to work for someone else. I had taken my children to Wednesday night Bible study and I decided, instead of attending the women's study, to find a quiet spot in the lobby and use that time for mental recovery. It had been a long day. I found a table in the lobby, put my head down, and began to deal with my thoughts and feelings about my job, my life, and the sense of enmity between the two. Employment is just not my thing! Yes, I know – nobody likes to work, and given the opportunity, we would all choose to give our employers the peace sign and spend our 9-5 on the beach somewhere. But it's much deeper than that for me. I believe God designed me to be an entrepreneur, not an employee. My purpose, my personality, my passion for life and for helping others are inextricably connected to entrepreneurship, and any time that I have found myself needing a traditional full-time job, I experience a serious internal conflict. Don't get me wrong – I'm not adverse to working in general. I am grateful for every job I've held, and have been blessed to excel in all of them. It's just that working as an employee rather than the business woman I'm called to be is out of character for me. It's out of alignment with the path God has predestined for my life. Consequently, having to go to a job everyday feels like I'm dying a slow, agonizing death.

As I sat in the lobby that August evening talking to the Lord, venting my frustrations of feeling trapped in someone else's standard, I blurted out the words, "I want to live boxed out!" After assuring the person across from me that I hadn't gone off the deep end, I began to write down what was transpiring in my mind: Why am I in a box? Why do we live in boxes? Why do we go through the motions every day rather than living out our purposes? Why do we limit what God can do? Why is it so easy to believe in God's greatness when it comes to everything and everyone else, yet much more difficult to believe He'll do the miraculous in our own lives? Why do we settle for the status quo when God is ready, willing, and able to do "exceeding abundantly" above all that we ask or think? Why do we *not* pursue our calling?

There were tons of questions going through my head. Then the one answer – the hard truth - became clear. We as people mentally put boundaries around God. We tend to think of Him in terms of our reality rather than basing our reality on Him. In other words, we look at our lives, our desires, our circumstances and take things at face value. We subconsciously accept the false notion that what we see is all there is to be seen. We resign to the mindset that says, "This must be all that God has for me. This is my world, this is what I know, this is what I see. I trust in the Lord to be with me - right here in this box. This is my life, so this must be where God is going to do His work." As a result, we try to make Him fit into our boxes with us, where it's comfortable and reasonable and easy for others and ourselves to accept. We feebly attempt to squeeze an uncontainable God into the confines of our own lives and rationale rather than tearing down the walls in our world and living like children of the God who spoke the universe into existence. I don't think we make a conscious decision to live in a state of confinement or to look at life through a limited lens. We're just routinized to the point of complacency. We have grown to look at life from our perspective only, which is bound to render a somewhat distorted view. What we should be doing is striving to see the world from God's perspective. This is the premise of living boxed out.

Have you ever seen those weird sciency glasses with the different colored lenses – you know, the red, green and blue ones that you can flip down over the clear lens so you can see different things? (Nicholas Cage wears them in the movie National Treasure). Well, we tend to walk around with our clear-lensed glasses on, seeing our lives only as they present themselves to the natural eye. We focus on what we can see – our surroundings, our circumstances, our abilities – and, good or bad, accept them as such. What we need to do is flip down the "God lens" over our eyes and then take another look around. That's where things get interesting! You'll begin to see things you didn't even realize were right in front of you. You'll do things that you never thought were possible. Your whole perspective on the world will change. You may care more about others, work harder, play more or have deeper faith. Life changes when you're looking at it from the angle of the One who created everything. An aerial view is always more vast and grand than the view at ground level.

Realizing the futility of my effort to make God fit into my view and into my world is what caused me to blurt out in the church lobby that night. It was time for me to do something different - to believe bigger. I needed to take my dissatisfaction with life as I knew it and use it as fuel to live on purpose. It was time for me to experience the fullness of life in Christ. I needed a fresh perspective and a new attitude. I needed to take a look at the world around me – my own little world – and recognize what could be helping or hindering my desire to not only do the work God called me to do, but to see *Him* differently. I realized that I needed to get out of my box. And so do you.

What's In Your Box?

So what exactly is this "box" I'm referring to? Simply put, the word "box" is a metaphor for your life. It is a figurative way of describing the people, routines, mindsets, actions, and experiences that make up your everyday world. Your box represents your present reality. It includes the tangible things that you see around you, such as your home, car, clothes, and places you go, as well as the intangible things, like your memories, habits, and emotions. Essentially, **your box is the collection of physical, mental, and emotional interactions between you and the world around you.** Your box is not inherently good or bad – it's simply the facts. As the saying goes, "It is what it is."

To live boxed out means not being satisfied with, "it is what it is." It means not accepting your life at face value, but being willing to see that there is so much more waiting for you and more for you to do.

Living boxed out means viewing your life in the context of God's boundless nature – rather than confining Him to the context of your life – and faithfully carrying out the work He has called you to do.

There is a world out there for you to leave an imprint on which far exceeds the radius of your current sphere of influence, and the only way for you to make an impact is by getting out there. You can't see the world, let alone affect it for Christ, when you're in a box. You have to open your eyes so you can see life from a wider point of view and be willing to open yourself to new possibilities and experiences. The King of the Universe has entrusted you with talents and abilities to utilize in the building of His kingdom and, through Him, you have access to an unlimited supply of everything you need to complete your assignments: discernment, strength, wisdom, connections, and resources - all without measure. If that doesn't make you feel empowered, I don't know what will!

Living boxed out means walking like your Father owns the cattle on a thousand hills — because He does! It means making the mental shift to prayerfully proceed in your purpose and move beyond anything that would prevent, deter, contain or otherwise keep you from acting out your faith to complete the specific work God has for you to do. No, this is not me telling you to quit your job, shuck your responsibilities and take a sabbatical in the wilderness somewhere so you can contemplate the meaning of life and sing Kum-ba-ya with the village children (unless, of course, you are certain that's what the Lord told you to do!).

What I am telling you is to earnestly desire God's will for your life and be willing to do whatever it takes to see it through. I'm still working full-time as I write this book, much to my chagrin, but now I understand that my employment status doesn't negate my purpose. God has things for me to do and, whether I work full-time, part-time, no time or until the end of time, His desire is that I live within His will and complete *His* work. My calling and your calling don't get cancelled out because of our circumstances. The onus is still *on us* to complete our assignments, even if that means we have to work a little harder to make that happen.

Living boxed out is a lifestyle, not just a catchy phrase. It's a way of being. It's about making a choice to assume your rightful place in God's master plan. You may not realize it, but you are quite valuable and very much needed in the grand scheme of things. The kingdom needs you. The world needs you. Even I need you. Although you and I may never actually meet, what you do – or don't do – with the assignment God has given you has implications that ripple through time and space, impacting the lives of people in your circle and the world at large. Yes, you are that important! Your gifts and talents were given for you to play a part in God's plan that only you can play, along with every other believer who has their part to play. When we do, we become a harmonious orchestra of purpose, and the music of our lives becomes a melody in the Conductor's ears. It's up to Him to work all things together for our good, but it's up to us to give Him something to work with! He trusts us with gifts and talents, but do we trust Him enough to step outside of our comfort zone and use them? This is what a boxed out life looks like – one completely reliant on God to be who He says He is, while fervently *doing* what He says we are to do.

I realize this whole concept is new and, trust me, living boxed out is a process. It may take time to open your eyes to the magnitude of God's greatness and to accept that His ability to accomplish great things doesn't just apply to everyone else. It applies to <u>you</u> as well.

Repeat after me: "God can and WILL do great things through me, because He is great and I am His." That's the first part of the process – believing bigger. Next, you'll have to accept the calling you've either been ignoring or unaware of, and you will need to deal with the things in your life that are inhibiting your forward movement. The reward comes when you remove those walls and discover that you have already been provided with the tools needed to do the work God has for you to do. You'll be energized and have a clearer perspective, which will propel you forward in planning and doing what you've been equipped to accomplish for the Lord. You'll be well on your way to living boxed out.

The seven chapters that follow represent the stages of a boxed out life. They describe the steps in the process of discovering and completing our God-given assignments. For illustrative purposes, the stages are presented here individually and in sequential order to help you identify where you may be at any given point in your life. However, in reality, these stages could overlap. If you have multiple assignments going on, you could find yourself in different stages at the same time, depending on the assignment itself or your response to it. In any case, the seven stages not only depict what believers go through in our Christian journey to doing God's will, they will provide practical insights and strategies to help you accomplish it.

1 - Believe Bigger

You alone are the Lord; You have made heaven, the heaven of heavens, with all their host, the earth and everything on it, the seas and all that is in them, and You preserve them all. The host of heaven worships You.
Nehemiah 9:6

There is no better place to begin than with God. After all, He is the Creator of all things. The universe only exists because He said so. The galaxies and planets revolve and rotate without chaos because He commanded them to do so. God has no beginning or ending. He created time and, therefore, isn't bound by it. He is not bound by space, either. He is fully everywhere at the same time. He is all knowing, which means He is keenly aware of everything that there is to know - ever. And He is omnipotent. He's all powerful and almighty. There is absolutely, positively nothing that He cannot do.

These attributes of God are difficult - actually impossible - for our finite minds to fully grasp, but it is important to stop and think about who God is so that we have a better understanding and acceptance of who we are in Him. We can't begin the conversation about our calling unless we come to terms with the One who's calling us. When we start to think about, I mean, really take time to ponder how utterly amazing God is and all of the vastly incredible things He has done, we have no choice but to acknowledge that He is just too much!

One simple way to get a glimpse of God's greatness is to take a good look around you. Nature is the very handiwork of God. Every day, everywhere we look, nature shows us what He has done, how majestic He is, and how boundless He is. Step outside on a clear night and look up at the stars. Not only did He create each star, but He made each one different, and He knows the name of every single star in the sky[1]. Have you ever been on an airplane? When you're soaring above the clouds, miles above the earth below, you can take a look out the window and see an endless expanse of fluffy, white beauty that makes you release the cares of the world below and gaze in awestruck wonder. Talk about a different perspective!

Another way to remind yourself of God's limitless character is one of my favorites – going to the beach. I grew up in Ohio, so my beach memories make me think more of kitty litter than God's greatness, but I digress. Now that our family has relocated to North Carolina, I'm just a few hours' drive away from the ocean…with real sand. I love to sit and stare out at the waters, whose end my eyes can't see. Looking out far enough, the sky and ocean seem to meet in a perfectly straight line of beautiful blue. I am amazed by the fact that God knows how many grains of sand are on that beach under my toes, along with every other grain of sand on all the other beaches of the world. He created every fish and creature swimming in the ocean. God the Son not only walked upon the waters, but controlled them by His voice[2]. How mind boggling is that? And that's exactly my point!

God *is* more and can *do* more than our minds can even take in. We can't process His works, make sense of them or even explain them in a way that does them justice. We don't even have the vocabulary at our disposal to articulate God. And that's OK, because there is something we can do. We can accept that He is greater than our capacity to comprehend. We can choose to believe that God is who He says He is. We can trust what He shows us of Himself in nature. We can take Him at His Word, because it's impossible for Him to lie. We can choose to believe that God is uncontainable. We cannot make Him fit into our box, because there's just too much of Him to fit in there. Our boxes aren't big enough to hold an infinite God. But we can certainly get out of our boxes and bask in His greatness. We can live in the knowledge of who He is, and rely on His power to do the things He has called us to do.

A common expression says that God uses ordinary people to do extraordinary things. The Bible is full of examples of everyday people who were called by God and, by His power, accomplished the unimaginable. David conquered Goliath. Noah built an ark and repopulated the earth. Gideon defeated an army. Moses led the Israelites from Egypt. Esther saved her people. Nehemiah rebuilt the Jerusalem wall. Peter spearheaded the growth of the church. Paul raised a man from the dead. These are all incredible accounts of how God used normal people to do wondrous works in His name.

What we see in each of these stories are people who weren't perfect. Not all of them had perfect responses to God's calling, but what they did have was faith in the God who called them. Some had doubts in their own abilities or worthiness, but none of them questioned God's ability. They trusted that if He called them, then He was able to strengthen and deliver them. They believed - regardless of their own hang-ups or other people's opinions – that God was capable of doing big things with major impact, so they acted in faith and obedience.

We read about the amazing things God has done in the Bible and we believe them to be more than mere stories, but actual historical events that show us just how mighty and powerful and merciful God is. Fast forward a couple thousand years and today, we still see Him do amazing things in people's lives. For example,

> God doesn't just want to use everyone else. He wants to use you.

think of the stories you've heard about people being healed of cancer or delivered from their deathbeds. Think about people who have walked away from horrible accidents completely unscathed or of marriages that were once on the brink of divorce that have been reconciled. Or people you went to school with who may now be famous or doing things on a very large scale. We see and hear these amazing things with our own eyes and ears – hardcore evidence that God is still alive and full of wondrous working power. We witness the great things He is doing all around us, and we have no problem believing that God is "showing up and showing out" in the lives of these ordinary people. We are moved by their stories, celebrating and thanking God right along with them. But things change when it's about us.

When it comes to ourselves, we don't always have that same level of confidence and expectation. We praise and shout over other people's testimonies and then shrink into doubt when it's time to believe that God wants to do the miraculous in our own lives. We sometimes have a hard time reconciling the power of God with our own perceived limitations and worthiness. Sure, we believe that He *can* do great things, but often struggle with believing that He *will* do great things for *us*.

God, the great I AM, is the same yesterday, today, and forever. His power does not sway with the times.

His ability is not based on our comprehension of it. He still does the miraculous, and He will do great things through you. He still uses ordinary people to do extraordinary things. You are one of His people and you have to know that God wants to use you – and the talents He's given you – to do His work. Like the people in the Bible, you only need to be a willing vessel for the carrying out of God's plans. The combination of His will and your willingness is a recipe for greatness.

So believe bigger. Believe that He is without limits in His love for you and in His power to do far more than you could ask or imagine. Believe that His miraculous ability to do much with little doesn't only apply to characters in the Bible or people that you know, but it applies to you as well. When you give your "little" to God, He takes it and multiplies it to bless the masses. You may never know if the result of your work will affect one person or millions, but whatever you do for the Lord is significant and, in God's hands, accomplishes wonders. Once you believe that, then you're ready to accept your assignment.

BELIEVE BIGGER → ACTIONS

1. Find a quiet space in your home or outdoors, turn off the technology, and contemplate an area of your life where you need to believe God "bigger."

2. Talk to the Lord about it. Ask for His help to see Him more clearly and to strengthen your faith.

2 - Accept Your Assignment

*Then He said to them, "Follow Me,
and I will make you fishers of men."
Matthew 4:19*

God, Creator of the universe, originator of life, Owner of all things, wants us to play a part in His Master plan. What an honor! He gives each of us gifts and talents that, when coupled with His wisdom and power, enable us to do great works. When Christians as a whole operate from our strengths and do the things God wants us to do, others can see the character and love of God displayed through us, which draws the world to Him and builds up other believers.

Living boxed out requires that you transition from just <u>believing</u> that God can do great things, to <u>acting out</u> that belief. You can do this by faithfully moving forward in His will for you. Without a doubt, you have work to do - which I call assignments. You may already know exactly what your assignment is or maybe you have no clue. Perhaps you're somewhere in between, having an inclination that God wants you to do something more, but you don't know specifically what that is. Whichever is the case, your primary means of gaining clarity comes from spending daily time with God in prayer, reading His word, and listening. God Himself is, by far, your best source for receiving instruction on what He wants you to do. He may send others along to confirm, affirm, or hold you accountable to what He has already instructed, but as His child, you have a direct line of communication to the Father. If you really want to know what He wants you to do, ask Him. He will let you know in His own way, in His time.

There are also some secondary cues that might help you recognize your calling. The Assignment Indicators™ on the following page may resonate with you and assist you in further identifying how God wants you to use your gifts and talents for the kingdom.

Assignment come in all shapes, sizes, and durations. You may have a talent for writing and believe you've been called to write poetry, books or blogs. Perhaps you're entrepreneurially minded and your assignment is to start a business, share your knowledge by teaching or hold a management position at your job. Or maybe you're the creative type and have the ability to craft works of art out of materials or melodies. Your assignment could be short term, such as stepping in for a neighbor who is sick and needs help getting her kids to school or helping the new guy at work get acclimated to his new position. It could also be long-term, such as assuming a leadership position at church or letting a family member live with you until they get back on their feet. Your assignment could be very public and visible or very private and seen only by God.

Assignment Indicators™
It *may* be your calling if:

- It seems to be inextricably linked to your very existence. If you're not doing it, you feel incomplete.
- It gives you a sense of meaning and peace.
- When you look back over your life, you see traces of your adult self, operating in your gifts in your past, even in your childhood.
- Others come to you for help in your area of expertise or gifting. You may even wonder *how* they know.
- You feel good doing what you do, even when the outcomes aren't what you expect.
- You can find a connection to your calling in whatever you do, including volunteer roles, extracurricular activities, clubs/organizations, and possibly employment or business ownership.
- It really isn't about you at all.
- It doesn't feel like work or trouble to you. You find pleasure in it.
- You can function in your calling well and effectively without having had any training, college education or instruction in it.
- It does not create or continue a life of imbalance.
- You dream and/or daydream (vision) about it.
- You can't seem to walk away from it, no matter what you do and no matter how much it challenges you.
- It does not measure its success against traditional standards.
- It doesn't contradict biblical principles.

You may be called to one task at a time or have several concurrent assignments. Your assignment could be within the walls of the church, at a school, in a prison, a hospital, in the community or in your own home. The possibilities are truly endless. Whatever your assignment is, you need to know for yourself that it is God-ordained and then you must respond accordingly.

Your part in God's plan is unlike anyone else's. Your special blend of gifts and talents make you uniquely qualified and positioned to complete the assignments He has preordained for you. That's right, God knew in advance that you, specifically, needed to play a particular role in His master plan. Much like a screenwriter who, before the script is complete, knows the precise actor he wants to play the starring role, God preselected you. He knows exactly who you are and what you can do. He knows your strengths and your weaknesses. He knows your personality and your proclivities. He knows what makes you laugh, what excites you, what motivates you, and what shuts you down. He knows your high notes and your hang ups. He knows all about your successes as well as your shortcomings. He knew your ending before you were even born, and in spite of what you think are failures, He loves you like a son or daughter. He loves you so much that He has entrusted you with the task of carrying out the Father's business. In fact, it's *because* of who you are that He has given you your particular assignment.

No one can carry out your assignment but you. It was divinely crafted with you in mind, custom made to fit the precise circumstances of your life. <u>He chose you</u>. This is why you feel a deep sense of void when you are not living out the purpose God has ordained for you. You feel like something is missing. You feel incomplete, uneasy, and spiritually unsettled. You may fit one of the following profiles.

Profile A – The Resigned

To look at you from the outside, everything seems fine. You go to work, do your job, go to church, hang out with friends, watch the game, laugh, smile, and wave. You pay the bills as best as you can, engage with your family, and even help others with their problems. You take a look around at your life – your home, your family, job, health – and while you might like some things to be different, you generally don't have any major complaints. You've had a few pretty good ideas in the past, and you have dreams about things you'd like to do in your future. In fact, you think there's something bigger, something more that God wants you to do, but you've grown tired of trying to figure it out. After all, your past attempts didn't work out, so your quest to discover God's plan for you is pretty much over. You're stuck or stalled. You've given up - figured it wouldn't happen. You have tried and failed or haven't tried at all - and this drains the life out of you each and every day. On the surface, you look just fine. But on the inside, you're wasting away, feeling incomplete, empty, and unfulfilled. Unsatisfied and depressed, you go through the motions, but something is still missing. You're existing but you're not living.

Profile B – The Overachiever

Life is awesome! Sure, your life isn't perfect, but it's pretty close. You are doing the things that you enjoy and that have meaning to you and others. You may or may not work a traditional job outside the home, but what does that matter? The important thing is that you're busy for the Lord, doing good works, volunteering and serving others wherever you can. If there were a checklist of things Christians should be rewarded for, you would feel pretty good about yourself: Attending church? Check! Giving tithes? Check! Serving in ministry? Check! What could be better?

Well, how about that nagging emptiness you feel each night when all of your do-goodness is over? What about the pestering realization that it's still not enough? There's something inside of you that just isn't fulfilled or complete, no matter how many roles you serve or how well you fill them. You've been so busy doing good deeds that you never stopped to think about the deeds you *should* be doing. And while you may not be aware of what your specific calling is, you do know one thing… life right now isn't truly that awesome, after all.

Profile C – The Runner

You know exactly what God wants you to do. You've either always known or you've recently discovered what your assignment is. There may have been people who have told you over the years that you have a gift or a calling - people who have spoken positively into your life and are sitting back expecting to see you do amazing things. In fact, you believe this about yourself as well. But you're running. You know your assignment but have not accepted it. You have your reasons - feelings of inadequacy or unworthiness, not wanting to make the changes in your life required to pursue your calling or feeling that those on the receiving end don't deserve what you've been assigned to do. You think you're flying under the radar and if you play it low-key enough and go on about your business, God will somehow forget that you're supposed to be about <u>His</u> business. You think you've escaped by running and hiding, but the truth is you're exhausted and drained, mentally and spiritually. Not only that, but your running has resulted in Jonah-like days spent in a dark, foul, belly of a fish, when you could be experiencing the fullness and blessings that come from doing God's will.

The common theme in each of these profiles is the lack of fulfilment caused by not living a life of purpose and obedience. Knowing that God has things for you to do (and we all do), yet not taking action to discover or do those things is nothing short of disobedience - and that's not where His blessings dwell. That's why, no matter how you try to forget about, cover up, or run from your assignment, you'll always feel like the people in the profiles above – incomplete and unfulfilled. But that's not how your story ends.

It doesn't matter to Him how many times you've tried and messed up. Or how long you've been running in place doing good things or flat out running away. Because of God's great love for you, He showers you with grace and mercy. He doesn't hold your past against you; He doesn't even see it. He sees who you are in His Son and He is ready to restore you. The void you have been experiencing can be filled. The peace you've been craving in the innermost part of your soul is available to you. Your Father is waiting with open arms to help you stand up, dust yourself off and grab the script, because you've got a role to play.

> *You are important to God.*

Having an awareness and understanding of what God wants you to do is pivotal. This knowledge should excite you, inspire you, and compel you to begin the work He's called you to. Knowing your assignment is fundamental, because you cannot do what you don't know you should be doing. However, once you know, you are officially held accountable for doing.

So how do you get there? How do you bridge the gap between believing God is who He says He is, that He has an assignment for you, and completing that assignment? The solution is a matter of choice. You must choose to believe that God will empower you to do His work and that He will be with you all the way. You must choose to accept that you are important to God, and believe the assignment He has given you is important to the kingdom. No matter what has kept you from moving forward in the past, you must decide to relish in the fact that each day is filled with new mercies and new opportunities. You must choose to live boxed out – break free of the status quo and step out into the world of purpose to which God is calling you. You must also be willing to address the barriers that have been keeping you boxed in, which we will cover in Chapter 3.

ACCEPT YOUR ASSIGNMENT → ACTIONS:

1. Re-read the Assignment Indicators. Grab a notebook and jot down 1-3 things that you believe God is calling you to do.

2. If you are willing, share your assignments with me by commenting on a special blog post titled "What's Your Assignment?" at **www.LiveBoxedOut.com**. I would be honored to read and pray over your list, that God will give you clarity and wisdom regarding what He wants you to do.

3 - Demolish Your Walls

*Yet in all these things we are more than
conquerors through Him who loved us.
Rom. 8:37*

That night in the church lobby when I declared that I wanted to live boxed out, God showed me the true source of my frustration and lack of contentment - and it wasn't at all what I expected it to be. I had approached Him that evening with my own flawed perception that my turmoil had to do with going to work for someone else, but He showed me that my issue wasn't about my employment situation at all. It was actually much deeper than that. My inner unease was the result of not living on purpose – not completing the work He had given me to do – regardless of whether I was employed full time, part time or no time. Talk about an awakening!

For the prior three years, I had all but given up on rebuilding my consulting practice. It flourished in Ohio, but it fizzled out not long after relocating. And after experiencing previous success, I just couldn't wrap my head around why my efforts weren't working this time. So after a period of dead ends and head-banging, I quit trying. I figured it must not be what God intended for me to do here. After all, things weren't going as well as they did before and certainly weren't going the way I thought they should. But right there in the church lobby, God let me know that the root problem wasn't my job. It wasn't even my business. It was me and my box. I wasn't seeing beyond my circumstances. I kept repeating the same actions, expecting something different to happen. And when it didn't, I thought that was it. I didn't see bigger at the time. I didn't see beyond the things that were blocking my view of God's ability to do infinitely more than I was doing. I was boxed in.

Like boxes in the literal sense, the boxes in our lives are made up of walls. Walls represent the things that prevent us from experiencing the freedom and empowerment that only come from choosing to pursue God's plan for us and doing the work He's given us to do. Walls are purpose-prohibitive. They block our view of the unlimited nature of God and cause us to focus on our own limitations. If you look at a standard cardboard box, you will notice that it has no windows or openings. This makes sense, right? After all, that box is meant to hold or deliver its contents without revealing what's inside. There is no view in and no view out - only containment. Walls are also restrictive of movement. Whatever is inside of that box is meant to stay exactly where it is, not moving around or spilling its contents all over the place.

So it is with our lives – our boxes. The walls do nothing but keep us confined, unable to see God's abilities and how He wants to use His power in our lives. When we're boxed in, we can't visualize the possibilities of what He has in store for us. Walls keep us sealed in place, hindered from moving about freely in our calling and unable to spill the overflow of God's blessings onto others. Walls block the flow of life-giving oxygen rather than allowing us to inhale and be revived by the Breath of Life. And if we want to experience that life, we must be willing to take an honest look at ourselves and identify anything that has been keeping us confined in our boxes.

You have to be willing to acknowledge the walls that have been blocking you from believing bigger and carrying out your own assignment. You're the only one who can truly assess what your specific reasons are. Once you identify those barriers, make the decision that it's time for the walls to come crashing down around you. Peace, blessing, and joy await you outside of those walls. Purpose awaits you outside of those walls. If you want it – go get it! You can break through those walls and you will emerge victorious!

> *It's time for the walls to come crashing down around you.*

Demolishing walls will require time and hard work, but the end result will be well worth your efforts. It has to begin at the root cause of the problem, so look beyond what you see on the surface (for me, it was my job) to get to the true source of what's been keeping you boxed in. There are countless reasons, and I discuss some of the common barriers here in great detail, because tearing down walls is the pivotal point in your pursuit of purpose. Without removal of barriers, there can be no movement.

The Wall of Fear

Fear is the great immobilizer. It keeps us from moving forward, keeps us scared, frozen in place, stuck in our boxes and afraid to trust God's bigger picture. Fear is worrying about things that haven't happened yet or about repeating things that already have. Fear makes us hold on to what we believe - in our natural minds and faulty human understanding - will keep us safe and secure. Fear is loud and argumentative; it makes a very compelling case as to why we should stay boxed in. Fear is also instinctual, meaning we don't have to be taught how to be afraid. It's human nature and comes easy for us, if we allow it.

Faith, on the other hand must be learned and doesn't come so easily. As a matter of fact, it goes against the very grain of our sinful nature. We have to teach ourselves to trust, over and over again. Faith is not an instinct, it's a choice. It is an active daily decision to place your trust in something that you can't see, control or know in advance. Faith is accepting that your limited knowledge is merely a speck in the infinitesimal sea of God's wisdom. Fear and faith cannot coexist, so you have to take a stand to believe in God's perfect plan. Faith is the only effective way to drive out fear, and completing your assignment without faith is impossible.

The Wall of Routine

The Great Wall of Routine has kept many a Christian from proactively pursuing their purpose. Your life has a rhythm. You have your regular patterns, activities, and commitments. You have an idea of how your days and weeks need to flow and, generally speaking, you do your best to conform your life to that standard. You're comfortable with how things are. It works for you and you don't want anything to come along and rock your box. Taking on something new would be....different. Well, different is a lot better than disobedient. Be careful not to let your comfort with the status quo keep you from hearing and receiving your next assignment.

The Wall of Wasted Time

Wasted time is one of the biggest barriers to being spiritually productive. Smartphone games and apps are major time wasters - particularly those involving candy, pets, sports, words, jewels, ninjas, zombies or birds (trust me, I'm stepping on my own toes here. I probably could've finished this book long ago if it weren't for those pesky games!). What about you? On any given day, how many hours do you spend swiping and tapping on your screen, spaced out in meaningless activity? Be honest with yourself. What else *could* you accomplish with that time?

You know what's next: TV. Over the past few years, television series have become more addictive than ever, thanks in part to the rise of social media. You can literally spend hours each night watching TV! Then, afterwards, you have carry-over conversations on Facebook™ about what happened to your favorite character. You may say it's just TV and it's really not that serious. Okay, "Not that Serious." I challenge you, for just one week, to tally the hours you spend watching and talking about your TV shows. Then compare that time with how much you've spent in prayer, reading the Word or developing that great idea God gave you. If you are a believer, everything is that serious. Distractions don't come with flashing lights and warning signs saying, "Hey Christian, don't watch me, don't touch me – I can keep you from doing the work God has for you to do!" No, distractions come wrapped up in things that appeal to your interests, that look good to you, sound good to you, keep you entertained, and ultimately, keep you unfocused and unproductive. You think you're just watching TV or playing games, but in reality, you're the one being played. Wake up, get up, and spend just one of those hours doing some of God's work, and see what a difference it makes in your life.

The People Wall

Yes, I am going there. There are some people in your life who are impeding your progress in purpose, and you really need to consider who those people might be. I'm not telling you to blame your spouse for all that's wrong in your world, or write someone off because you feel they're the culprit behind your void. What I am suggesting is that people will either encourage us and propel us forward in God's work or discourage and hold us back. There is no neutral ground. Be willing to look at the people in your life and assess which side of the scale they're standing on. Is there someone who seems to always speak negatively and is constantly complaining? They never seem to have anything positive to say! I've met people who, on a bright, sunny, summer day would be the one to spot a few clouds far off in the distance. Negative people are draining and it's okay to put some space between you and them, lest their perspective becomes your own and they cause you to question what God really wants you to do.

Are you spending so much time with someone that there's no time left for God? Maybe you really enjoy spending lots of time with them (or maybe they're very needy), but at what cost? Could you exchange some of that time for time with God or on His purposes?

Is there someone whose opinion you place so much value on that what they say holds more weight than what God requires? Everyone thinks they know what's best for you and what you should be doing with your life and sometimes those opinions can weigh you down. Opinionated people tend to be vocal and loud, while God often speaks to us in a still, small voice. It's hard to hear Him when people are yelling their opinions in your ear.

On the other hand, you may have people in your life who nourish your soul. They support you spiritually and emotionally. They are givers, not takers, and your relationship with them is mutually rewarding. They listen to you, bring you joy, lift your spirit when you're down, laugh with you, and hold you accountable to who you are in Christ. They encourage you, and their presence in your life energizes you to carry out your calling.

There will always be people in our boxes with us. We don't live on a deserted island and God didn't design us to be alone. He wants community with us, and He wants us to have fellowship with others. People can be a blessing, but be mindful not to let people become a barrier to what God has for you. The key is to examine your existing relationships and how they are helping or hindering your response to what God has given you to do. If your relationship with God is intact and top priority, meaning you spend time with Him on a regular basis, then He will give you discernment regarding your other relationships.

The Wall of Excuses

This, by far, is the most common deterrent to living boxed out. It's a bit oxymoronic that we want our lives to be better, yet sabotage our own efforts before we even get started. It's like saying you want to lose weight, but in the same breath say that you don't have time to exercise and you like sweets too much to give them up. Well, which is it? Do you want to lose weight or do you want to enjoy sweets and stay as you are – or possibly get into worse shape? You can't have it both ways, no matter what type of 100-calorie pack or other alternative, "healthier" junk food you choose. Living boxed out is no different. You can't say that you believe in God's power to do great things in your life and that you accept your role in making that happen while simultaneously listing all the reasons why you can't do your part. It just doesn't work that way. You can either pursue what He wants you to do or be man/woman enough to get on your knees and come clean with the Lord about why you think you can't accept your assignment, so that He can dispel those excuses and empower you to get up and move forward.

What are your excuses? What have you told yourself are the reasons you can't move forward in your calling? You cannot tear down this wall if you don't first acknowledge that the wall is there. I challenge you right now to write down all the things you have said to yourself or even vocalized to someone else about why you can't do the work God wants you to do or why you can't pursue that idea He's placed in your heart. I want you to see on paper what has been keeping you in your box. You need to be honest enough with yourself to own your excuses if you want to move beyond them. You've crutched on them all this time, so don't back down now.

Now, you listen and listen good. If you don't get anything else from this book, I need you to hear and take this to heart: God is bigger than any of your

> *God is bigger than any of your excuses, issues or what-ifs*

excuses, issues or what-ifs. If your excuse starts with the word "too" – too young, too old, too tired, too late, too nervous, too much – then it's time for you to replace those phrases with, "God is too powerful to fail and He loves me too much to leave me hanging." He will be there, right by your side, to help you do whatever He has inspired you to do. If your excuses contain the words "not enough" – not smart enough, not skilled enough, not a good enough speaker, not popular enough, not social enough, not experienced enough – then it's time that you start believing that there are not enough reasons in the world to keep God from empowering you to do His work. The mere fact that He has called you means that the work is already destined to be completed. All you need to do is believe that God knows all about you and your issues, yet He still loves you and He chose you to do this work. Take that list of excuses you wrote down and present them to the Lord on your knees in prayer. Know that He's got your back and that His grace and provision cancel out all those excuses. Now get up and get moving. There's no more time for pity parties.

The Wall of Busyness

Have you ever met someone who is always busy, but busy doing good things? It seems they are constantly involved in a project, ministry, service opportunity, helping someone, keeping their kids engaged in a sport or activity, volunteering here, helping there. They seem to never grow weary in well-doing. Maybe I've just described you. It is possible to do too much, even when it's good stuff. God does want and expect us to serve others, but He also expects us to maintain order and balance in our lives. And above all, He expects us to serve Him. Don't let your pursuit of doing good things keep you from doing the best thing, which is the work He's called you to do. Ask yourself why you're doing all the things you're doing. Are you staying busy all the time to avoid dealing with another issue? Are you afraid that you might be held more accountable if you slow down long enough to hear what God is trying to say to you? Good things are good, but they are no substitute for purpose.

The Wall of Situations

Oftentimes, our present-day circumstances are restrictive and it can be challenging for us to see beyond them. These situations are temporary conditions or phases in life that we find ourselves in, either due to our own decisions or as the result of another's decisions or actions. Situations can be physical in nature (being in the hospital or starting school), emotional (stress or depression), relational (a new baby or marriage issues) or financial (unemployment or debt). The key issue here is assessing the situations in your life that you may be using as your assignment alibi. In other words, you tell yourself that because of a particular situation, you can't focus on or carry out your assignment.

There are some circumstances that call for a temporary shift in our focus away from our assignment so that we can deal with and bring closure to them. Doing so will actually make us more in-tune and effective in God's work. Just be sure to keep your focus on God as you deal with any situation, since He's the only one who can ultimately bring resolution and bring you back to the task at hand.

Situations are not always bad or negative. Sometimes things just are what they are - a part of your life that you'll have to learn to navigate, work around or work with in order to accomplish your mission. Children are an example. If you're a stay-at-home mom, single parent or working married parent with young children at home, then a great deal of your time and attention will be focused on your children - and rightfully so. They need your help with homework, preparing meals, refereeing sibling fights, and nurturing them when they are sick or hurt. They're young and they need you, but this is a situation you can learn to navigate, not one that you should allow to become an excuse for not moving forward in your purpose. Speaking from experience, I know this can be challenging, but not impossible.

One of my personal goals was to pursue a post-graduate degree. The situation? At the time, I didn't work outside the home, I had a very energetic toddler, a nursing newborn, no local family support, and a husband who worked third shift. My time was not my own! Yet, I trusted what God had in store for my future and fully embraced the truth of Philippians 4:13 which reminded me I can do all things through Christ who gives me strength. Sure, there were late nights, early mornings, and nursing-studying, sessions, but by the grace of God I walked across the stage and received my Master's – on time.

Whatever your situations are, view them in the context of an all-powerful God and they will look a lot smaller and a lot more feasible. Find ways to be purposeful and productive, even in your current situation. Make some changes, adjust your schedule, and tap into other people and resources for help. You can and will get through any situation when you rely on God, even when the going gets tough. And be careful not to let your situations become the building blocks for the Wall of Excuses.

The Wall of Things Past

Your past will certainly impede your future if you allow it to. There are many positive things that can be gleaned from our past that we can use as an aid for the work ahead, which we will examine in Chapter 5. However, this particular wall is about the not-so-positive experiences you may have had. Whatever is in your past – traumatic experiences, loss of a loved one, violence, addictions, financial bondage, bad decisions, hurtful people – it's time to let go. Where there is hurt, it's time to forgive. Where there is regret, forgive yourself. Understand that when God forgives, He actually forgets. According to His word, "as far as the east is from the west, so far has he removed our transgressions from us.[3]" There is nothing that you have done or have failed to do that God won't forgive. Where there are scars, it's time to accept your healing. Our miracle-working God doesn't just heal physical wounds, He can heal your emotional ones as well. There is nothing in your past that He can't deliver you from.

If you allow your past to keep you from accepting your assignment, then you have given the devil his victory. Don't give it to him. Stand on God's Word which says you are more than a conqueror in Jesus Christ and all things are possible through Him. Read and embrace His words. They offer you encouragement, hope, peace and proper perspective. You can incorporate the Bible into your life by memorizing scriptures that speak healing and deliverance. Write verses on index cards or sticky notes and place them around your home to remind you of God's love and power.

Additionally, to be released from your past, forgive those who have hurt you and ask for forgiveness where you have hurt others. If you've been through traumatic experiences, it may be necessary to seek counseling. There is no shame in counseling; God has placed people in these positions to help others. They're just professionals operating in their gifts, much like we aspire to operate in ours. Many free resources abound through churches and nonprofit agencies, and even some employers offer an employee assistance program (EAP) that could be helpful. Get out and connect with groups or individuals who will lift you up, and distance yourself from those who would try to keep you down by reminding you of who you used to be. There is a light at the end of your tunnel. His name is Jesus. He needs you to get unstuck from your past so you can enjoy the good future He has in store for you.

I understand that facing the walls in your life can be difficult and maybe even downright painful. Changing your TV or smartphone habits is one thing, but dealing with your past or possibly limiting your interactions with someone is another thing entirely. You will have to make some hard choices, but the choice has to be made. You can't stay where you are. You have to remove walls to get to the life God has for you. Some of those walls may come crashing down in an instant, as if you took a sledgehammer to them. In other cases, it may feel like you're trying to knock down a mighty wall with only a pick axe in your hands, crumbling just a little at a time. None of your walls will come down easily, but they can – and they must – come down, no matter what is required or how long it takes.

Your most effective tool for demolishing walls is prayer. I've said it previously and I'll continue to say that prayer is powerful and it works. God will either change the situation or change you in it, but your prayers are always heard and always answered. I encourage you to always start tearing down your walls in a kneeling position (or flat on the ground) – praying to the God who listens and responds. This position would never work in physical demolition, but when it comes to bashing walls, it works wonders. In addition, find other means and support systems to bolster you through this wall-busting stage. This is a perfect time to pair up with an accountability partner or prayer partner – someone you can join forces with, taking your concerns to the Lord together.

Once you have decided to pursue God's calling on your life, you have alerted the enemy that kingdom expansion is about to take place, and he is not pleased about it. Therefore, Satan is going to round up his travelling reconstruction crew to counter your wall demolition. Every effort you make to tear down the walls of your box will be countered by his attempts to bring in new and improved walls or patched up ones in order to keep you boxed in. His goal is to thwart any growth of the kingdom and to prevent any glory from being given to God through your life. But know this: while he may try to slow it down, he cannot stop God's plan. He is already defeated and he knows it. The devil may try to rebuild walls in your life to keep you from believing God and doing His work, but he is powerless in the presence of God who lives in you. You just need to understand what kind of battle you are in, and come prepared with the right weaponry to win.

Regardless of what your walls are – whatever your reasons for not accepting or acting on your assignment from God – you need to tear them down by inviting the Lord into the situation. Call on Him and stand on His Word. Speak His Word back to Him when you pray. I encourage you to start a notebook, journal, or even a box of index cards of verses that you can read and pray on throughout this demolition phase. Here are a few to get you started.

Stand firm then, with the belt of truth buckled around your waist, with the breastplate of righteousness in place, and with your feet fitted with the readiness that comes from the gospel of peace. In addition to all this, take up the shield of faith, with which you can extinguish all the flaming arrows of the evil one. Take the helmet of salvation and the sword of the Spirit, which is the word of God. And pray in the Spirit on all occasions with all kinds of prayers and requests. With this in mind, be alert and always keep on praying for all the Lord's people. (Ephesians 6:14-18)

No weapon forged against you will prevail, and you will refute every tongue that accuses you. This is the heritage of the servants of the Lord, and this is their vindication from me," declares the Lord. (Isaiah 54:17)

No, in all these things we are more than conquerors through him who loved us. (Romans 8:37)

The Lord is my rock, my fortress and my deliverer; my God is my rock, in whom I take refuge, my shield and the horn of my salvation, my stronghold. (Psalm 18:2)

I called to the Lord, who is worthy of praise, and I have been saved from my enemies.(Psalm 18:3)

In my distress I called to the Lord; I cried to my God for help. From his temple he heard my voice; my cry came before him, into his ears. (Psalm 18:6)

And without faith it is impossible to please God, because anyone who comes to him must believe that he exists and that he rewards those who earnestly seek him (Hebrews 11:6)

Jesus looked at them and said to them, "With man this is impossible, but with God all things are possible." (Matthew 19:26)

Your walls do not mark the end of your journey. They are nothing more than removable, temporary blockades that you can break through to get to the abundant life God wants you to experience. Even if your box is good, God still desires more from you and for you. Remember that you were chosen in advance to do good works for Him. Despite what may appear to be impassible walls in your way, you have within you the tools you need to not only destroy those walls, but to step over them like a heap of rubbish as you forge ahead into your destiny.

#3 – DEMOLISH YOUR WALLS → ACTIONS:

1. Identify 5 things that have been keeping you from moving forward in your assignment(s).
2. Write them on an index card, then destroy that card.
3. Find and memorize one Bible verse that will encourage and empower you to proceed.

4 -Take Inventory

For You formed my inward parts; You covered me in my mother's womb. I will praise You, for I am fearfully and wonderfully made.
Psalm 139:13-14a

After you decide to demolish the walls in your life and the dust begins to settle, you will find that things look different. Your perspective will be clearer and you should have a more complete, unobstructed view of yourself and the world around you. You will be better able to hear God's voice, softly and lovingly guiding you to your next steps. And you should feel differently, as there is something very liberating about tearing down walls. You came, you saw, you conquered! No longer are you confined to life as you knew it, but you are free to move about within the perfect will of God and pursue all that He has for you. You should feel unweighted and ready to journey with God out of your box and into your destiny.

As with any journey, you begin by considering what you might need for the road ahead. You assess what you currently have in your possession that you should take with you and make a list of what you might need to pick up along the way. This is also how you must begin to move forward in your assignment.

Taking inventory is an exercise of preparation. It is also a way to build yourself back up and fill your life with positive things after you've torn down those walls. Taking your own personal inventory means counting your assets and knowing what you have at your disposal that could facilitate the work ahead. Remember, if God called you to do something, He has already equipped you with everything you need to complete it. In a way that only He could divinely prearrange, you have already been given the essentials needed to successfully complete your assignment. You were chosen because you have what it takes.

> *God has preordained the work He has for you to do, and placed within you everything needed to carry it out.*

This is why taking inventory is so important. It is a way to be reminded of who God made you to be and how unique you are among the millions of His children. This process will help you see your real value as opposed to the worth someone else tries to place on you. The self-assessment aspect of counting your "assets" will cause you to discover that you are more prepared for the work ahead than you thought. Seeing what God has already placed within you will build your confidence and motivate you to move forward.

A good place to begin taking inventory is with your gifts, talents, and skills. Gifts, in the spiritual sense, are "special attributes given by the Holy Spirit to every member of the Body of Christ according to God's grace for use within the context of the Body.⁴" They include wisdom, leadership, administration, discernment, helps, and others. We each have gifts to use for the edification of the kingdom, and they are equally important. If you're not sure what yours are, see the back of this book for information about a free spiritual gift questionnaire.

Talents are the things that seem to come naturally for us and that we do exceptionally well. Singing and athleticism are popular examples of talents, but the possibilities are endless. My husband, for example, has a talent for analysis (and the gift of discernment). He can understand and process numbers, people, and situations quicker and more accurately than anyone I have ever met. There are some things I don't even bother trying to understand — I ask him and he translates for me. You may be talented in public speaking, artistry or planning events. Talents are not typically something we learn, which is why I personally believe that our talents are also given to us by God, much like our gifts. No matter how hard I wish to be a great singer or how loud I sing in my car, the truth is that I'm just not talented in that area.

Skills, on the other hand, can be learned. Skills are abilities that tend to involve knowledge or hands-on application. They're what I consider to be the real-life, practical capabilities that enable us to get work done. People skills, sewing, computer skills, and carpentry are a few examples. Skills, talents, and gifts are all vital tools on your quest to live boxed out and you will draw upon each of them as you move forward. I encourage you to make a list of yours so you can see just how fearfully and wonderfully made you are.

Beyond your gifts, talents and skills, there is so much more that you can count as a blessing and potential "asset." Think about your work experience. Regardless of your position or industry, look back over your career history and all the places you've worked. Every job presented an opportunity for you to learn something, connect with someone or garner some level of professional experience that could prove valuable to you in another area of your life, particularly in God's work. Were there words spoken to you by someone you respected that still influence you today? Were there software programs you learned or certifications you earned? Did you pick up any tips on business etiquette or professional networking or gain insight about other cultures?

Remember, nothing in life is without purpose. While opportunities may have come to you through your job, those experiences are now part of your personal inventory. Sift through your career and find what might come in handy for your next assignment. Reflect on your education and take note of knowledge gained from an academic setting that might serve you well, as you serve the Lord. Whether high school, vocational school, college, seminars or adult education, assess those educational opportunities and how they might help you now. What can you draw from those things you've learned? For example, several years ago, I was blessed to be able to spend two weeks in Washington, D.C. for an event management certification program. I completed the coursework, but did not actually complete the certification. However, I don't consider this a loss. I kept all of my course materials, notes, and textbook, and frequently draw on what I learned throughout the program to plan events for my clients – almost 20 years later! Learning is only meaningless if you don't apply it to your life.

Another way to assess your personal inventory is to look for any patterns and themes that may have emerged throughout your life. As you think back over the years, you may see traces of your gifts and talents being used in various scenarios in your younger life. This is actually a pretty cool process that God took me through, revealing to me how, even as a child, I had the makings of what He designed me to be as an adult. As a fourth grader at Sheridan Elementary, I was on top of the world. I loved school and had some pretty awesome friends. We had so much fun giggling, passing notes, and being uniquely ourselves. Our friendships extended beyond the school walls as we walked home together, went to each other's birthday parties and had sleepovers. Life was about as good as it could get, and I suppose the only way I knew to capture how awesome I felt was to start a club. It was called "Girls Are Great" or G.A.G. for short. Hey, don't judge me – I was 10! This was an invitation-only membership club, complete with ID cards and membership books and I was the president. To this day, I don't know what this club actually *did*, other than profess that we were great and boys were inferior. We didn't accomplish anything for the good of the school or girls as a gender, but none of that mattered. The point is, I was then who I am today – a leader with a gift in administration and talents in planning and organization. Granted, I didn't see this X number of years ago (LOL, you thought I would slip and reveal my age, didn't you!), but as a result of taking my own personal inventory, God showed me a theme that developed over the course of my life. That 4th grade club experience becomes much more significant when I line it up next to the times I facilitated Sunday School as a teenager, was voted president of the college gospel choir, held leadership roles in volunteer capacities and started my own business.

What themes can you spot in your own life? Discover them by taking your own personal inventory. Review your earlier years for trends in the roles you've played or activities you have consistently been drawn to.

What do friends and family most often come to you for help with? You may find clues there as well.

The themes you uncover show that there were seeds of your future purpose already planted in you, even as a child. They were actually there before you were born! As I've said before, God has preordained the work He has for you to do, and at the same time, placed within you everything needed to carry it out. Acknowledging who He made you is a form of praise, because you're thanking Him for taking the thought, love and care to make you just who you are. Reflect on your life and then thank God for what He has done in you, as well as what He will yet do through you.

Now that you have decided to live boxed out – more purposefully and intentionally – you should begin to feel excited and invigorated! You have decided to deal with the walls that have been keeping you boxed in for so long, and now you can see more clearly the bright future that awaits. You're full of optimism, energy, faith, and motivation. And after having tallied your assets and resources, you feel well-prepared to move forward in the assignment prepared in advance for you to do. You're ready to run full steam ahead into your purpose, and I applaud your tenacity! As you get ready to run, be sure to keep two things in mind: 1) Your inventory - your talents, experiences, gifts, and skills will be the fuel you need to keep going; and 2) Your plan - no journey should begin without a plan of how to get from start to finish. We'll cover planning in the next Chapter.

TAKE INVENTORY → ACTIONS

1. Visit **www.LiveBoxedOut.com** and download the free SWOT Analysis template.
2. Fill in the SWOT using yourself/your assignment as the basis.

5 - Plan for Success

There is a time for everything, and a season for every activity under the heavens.
Ecclesiastes 3:1 NIV

A college English professor was discussing a mid-semester writing assignment with his class. Unlike other papers the students had written earlier in the year, this particular essay would be worth 25% of their final grade. It was a big deal, so on this morning, the professor decided not to lecture as usual, but to focus on the requirements of the essay instead. He spent about 15 minutes giving the students a high-level overview, explaining how this assignment related to what they have read and written throughout the year. He concluded by announcing that he had prepared a detailed overview of the essay – his expectations, the framework for the essay, the grading criteria, and the deadline. Because this was such a large part of the students' grade, he told the class that he would distribute this overview in class the next day to provide further insight and open the door for a Q&A session. Then, class was dismissed.

An ambitious, intelligent student in this class felt she had a pretty good grip on what the professor wanted in this essay. After all, she had taken a couple of his English classes before and knew all about his grading style; she would always read the comments he wrote in red on her papers and adjusted her writing accordingly. Plus, he just gave an overview of the assignment, so she felt confident that she could at least get started on writing. Once she began, the words just seemed to flow and, before the night was over, she had written 17 pages on the subject, complete with citations. She saved her work, shut down her laptop for the night, and went to bed feeling quite accomplished.

The next morning, remembering that today's English class wouldn't be a lecture, she decided to skip it. She didn't need further review or to sit through a Q&A session. Her paper was done, and she could certainly use that hour to finish work for other classes. And so she returned to class the following day, instead. Eager to be commended by the professor, she walks in with the paper in her hand and smugly hands it to him. "Here's my essay," she gleams, "I wanted to get started right away, and the words just seemed to come to me, so I was able to get it done early. I know that you have specific expectations for our writing, and I believe I was able to capture them here." The professor takes the paper as she stands and waits. He flips through the pages, nodding his head and glancing at her occasionally with a crooked smile. She thinks "Oh yeah, I've *got* this." The professor looks up at her and says, "You are right. This is a very well written paper." She is all but bursting at the seams! "But this is not at all what I wanted, nor is it what I assigned. Were you not in class yesterday?" "No...I, uh, already had this written and figured I didn't need to come." The professor replied, "If you would have been present, you would have received the full details of this assignment, in which I clearly laid out my expectations. You see, this particular assignment is a class effort. I intend to take your individual essay and compile it with the other students' to create a writing portfolio for future classes. Because this is an advanced class, your paper will be an example of my teaching to other students for years to come." She hung her head and apologized, ready to accept an F. "Here," the professor said, "You are one of my most ambitious students and best writers, which is why you were selected for this assignment." She looks up, "But I thought we all had to write about the same thing?" "No, each student is unique and I chose their assignments based on their personalities, writing styles, and ability to deliver what I was looking for. No two papers will be the same. This is so future students can have a better picture of me as a professor and what they can receive from taking my class." "I guess this means I failed, then," she concedes. "No. I will not grade this paper," he says, handing the essay back to her. "But I do expect you to attend class everyday so that you can receive my instructions and complete the assignment based on my plans, not your assumptions." She takes her paper, grateful for another chance, and sits down to hear what's in store for today.

And so it is with us. Our assignments come from God. He inspires us with ideas and gives us vision. He expects us to use our common sense to figure out some of the details, but He has the ultimate say-so regarding what the assignment is, as well as how and when to complete it. He is the One who holds the guidelines, reviews your work, and when it's all said and done, gives you feedback on how you utilized your talents. Therefore, it's in your best interest to show up to class and pay attention to what the Master is saying. Be present with Him. Your successful hearing, understanding, and completion of the work God has for you depends 100% on your "attendance" in His presence. There's no way you can expect to proceed in the Lord's work – remaining in His will - without receiving instruction from Him first. John 15:5 states, "I am the vine, you are the branches. He who abides in Me, and I in him, bears much fruit; for without Me you can do nothing." You must spend time daily in prayer, in listening, and in reading of His instruction manual – the Bible. Doing so will ensure that you complete your assignment to God's expectations and not your own assumptions.

God is the Master Planner. He doesn't just see big picture, but the entire picture. He knows the beginning, ending, and everything in between. You, on the other hand, do not! It's not your job to know the end result of your assignment or how it fits into God's plan. Sometimes we don't take steps forward because we don't know what the outcome will be. We can't see how it will all play out, so we are hesitant to even get in the game. Not knowing can be tough, especially for us Type A personalities who want to know all the details so we can plan out the next three years. But when it comes to matters of faith, you're going to have to accept that you may not be shown the big picture. You may not know what will happen after you complete your assignment or how impactful it will be, and that's okay. He may reveal these things to you, but He may also show you only what you need to know right now. Trust His plan, and be content with knowing and doing your part. Believe that God's *got this.*

While trusting in God, His wisdom, and His plan, you are responsible for completing your role in that plan by doing the work God has called you to do. Completing your assignment should be intentional, with careful thought and planning to the extent you can. Planning is a concept and practice instituted by God Himself (despite what time management gurus would have you think), and the Bible communicates to us how important planning is.

> *Trust God's plan and focus on doing your part.*

Luke 14:28-29 states,

> *"Suppose one of you wants to build a tower. Won't you first sit down and estimate the cost to see if you have enough money to complete it? For if you lay the foundation and are not able to finish it, everyone who sees it will ridicule you"*

And Proverbs 21:5 tells us,

> *"The plans of the diligent lead to profit as surely as haste leads to poverty."*

Embarking on the Lord's work, no matter what it is, should be taken seriously enough to do it the right way – His way. God's way is one of order, not haphazard actions. As you prepare to complete your assignments, exercise your mind, your personal inventory, and the resources at your disposal to develop a course of planned actions.

Creating a plan for accomplishing your work requires that you consider the various aspects of <u>what</u> you have to do, along with when, how, who, and what you need to do it. Some assignments may require detailed, written plans, such as a business plan for starting a business. "Smaller" assignments (in quotes because I don't believe any are small) may require a much simpler approach and less time to work through. However, a plan is still necessary, regardless of the magnitude of the assignment. The planning process causes you to think through all of the factors involved, which results in wiser and more calculated actions. Planning also sets you up to succeed in the completion of your work, because it forces you to foresee any potential roadblocks and to develop a contingency plan in the event things don't go as expected. Every good plan should include a strategy for managing potential hiccups.

The act of planning isn't as daunting or as difficult as it sounds. Keep the process simple. Just answer the five Ws that you learned in school (who, what, where, when, why – and how), and you'll be fine. Don't make the planning process so complex that it becomes a wall, impeding your progress rather than moving you forward. Once you know your assignment, you have the basis for your plan. The details come by staying connected to God, acting on the insights He gives you, and adjusting as you go along. The rest of the planning process involves three basic yet fundamental elements: research, writing, and counsel.

Plan for Success: RESEARCH

Research is one of my least favorite activities in all of creation, but it is necessary. Research, in its most basic definition, means to gather information. If you've ever gone online to find a recipe for a meal you wanted to prepare or watched a video on how to fix something, then you've conducted research. Researching is about collecting data that you can use to make sound, knowledgeable decisions.

Research is especially important when taking on something you've never done before or when dealing with assignments that are more complex in nature with various moving pieces to be considered and coordinated. For example, starting a business requires an extensive amount of research to assess the geographic area where you intend to offer your products or services, to get a gauge on your competitors, and to know which distribution channels will best serve your target market. If you are writing a book, you'll need to do some research before deciding whether to self-publish or to use a publishing company, and if the latter is the best choice, deciding which company to use. Adopting a child will require research not only to learn about the child's history, but which agency to use, what changes may need to be made to your home, what financial adjustments need to be made and how the process typically works in your state or county.

When conducting your research, utilize a variety of resources – trusted resources. The Internet is full of solid, useful information, but it's also chock full of junk and fabrications, so choose what you use wisely. Additionally, document where you find the information in case you want to go back and read more. The library, antiquated as some may view it, is still a great place to learn. Reading books, trade journals and reference materials will not just give insight for the work at hand, but will also keep those brain cells active, stimulating your overall thought process. Talk to real people who may be experienced or reputable experts in the area of work you're taking on. They may be more than willing to share resources or insights that helped them along the way. Every bit of information you gather will increase your awareness and serve as a starting point for sound decision making.

Plan for Success: WRITING

I'm a bit old fashioned when it comes to writing, in that I prefer pen and paper over technology. Writing something down makes it more real. I feel more committed to it and I remember it better. Of course, this backfires when I leave my lists at home or head to the coffee shop to work and realize I've forgotten my notes. This is where technology comes has an advantage. Using a laptop, tablet or even your smartphone allows you to have cloud-based access to your notes. You can be productive anywhere with Internet access, which means you can convert down time (waiting at the doctor's office, airport, etc.) into productive time. Whichever method works for you - writing, technology or a combination of both - capturing your thoughts and documenting your research is a key component of planning.

The purpose of writing things down is to translate information from the intangible world of your mind to the physical world. Writing helps you organize your thoughts and sort through the information you have gathered. Writing is also a small way of making your assignment come to life. It mentally commits you to the work as you remove it from your imagination and put it on paper. Writing also helps you retain and recall the things you've learned.

What exactly should you write? Everything! For starters, you should write out the action steps it will take to get from where you are now (starting your assignment) to where you need to be (assignment completed).

> *Write the vision and make it plain on tablets, that he may run who reads it.*
>
> *– Hab. 2:2*

Develop a step-by-step strategy of how you will carry out the task before you. Set target dates and mini goals along the way so you can gauge your progress. This will give you something specific to strive for each day and will hold you accountable to yourself.

You should also write notes. If you're taking a class, jot down the important points. If something the pastor says really resonates with you, write it down. As you conduct research and begin to mentally shape the approach you want to take, write down your thoughts. If God gives you an idea at 3:00 in the morning, drag yourself out of bed or keep a notebook on your nightstand so you can write it down. The writing aspect of this planning phase is more about organizing your thoughts rather than creating a formal document. Writing is simply the output of your research, brainstorming, listening, and learning. Whether you use a notebook, laptop, tablet or journal, writing is essential for converting your ideas into actions.

Plan for Success: COUNSEL

The Bible makes it very clear that wisdom comes from seeking counsel. Unfortunately, this part of the planning phase is often overlooked or ignored. No one likes being told what to do! However, receiving advice is good and necessary on so many levels. It keeps us humble and helps us maintain the proper perspective that this assignment isn't about us. Counsel presents different viewpoints that we may not have otherwise considered. It also exposes us to knowledge that we might never gain on our own. Most importantly, seeking counsel is biblical. There are several passages of Scripture that speak to the importance of obtaining sound advice for life, planning, and decision making. A few of them are provided here:

> *Let the wise listen and add to their learning, and let the discerning get guidance (Prov. 1:5)*
>
> *The way of fools seems right to them, but the wise listen to advice. (Prov. 12:15)*
>
> *Plans fail for lack of counsel, but with many advisers they succeed. (Prov. 15:22)*

As you become more clear about your assignment from the Lord, seek out people with whom you can discuss your plans and who can give you solid input and advice. Look for someone who can be real with you - preferably someone who knows you and is in a position to give you spiritual guidance. Listen to them with an open mind and open heart, even if it means hearing something you might not want to hear. Good counsel isn't about consoling you; it's about helping you make the right decisions. Pray before your conversations with your counsellor (or mentor, friend, pastor, coach, etc.) and ask God to give you discernment regarding both the counsel and the person giving it. God will either confirm what He's told you in your quiet time or He may lead you in different direction.

Seeking counsel is not a quest to find someone to validate some crazy notion that you've come up with on your own. We sometimes fabricate our own thoughts about what we should be doing (rather than just doing what God said). We could have a great idea or long-standing ambition to do something that isn't necessarily the "what" God wants us to do. Then we go out and try to find scriptures and people to substantiate our idea. This is not what seeking counsel is about. This part of the planning process should be a purposeful pursuit of wisdom done with a heart that is ready to receive guidance, incorporating said guidance into your plan where appropriate and in alignment with your assignment. Wise counsel is the capstone of your planning process and, combined with the research and writing you've done, prepares you for the next stage of a boxed out life: Action.

PLAN FOR SUCCESS → ACTIONS

1. Find or purchase a notebook to be used only for ideas, notes, and research related to your assignment.

2. Think about who might be a good resource for giving you Godly counsel. Pray about it. Set up a time to chat with them.

6 - Work It Out

And let the beauty of the Lord our God be upon us, and establish the work of our hands for us; Yes, establish the work of our hands.
Psalm 90:17 NKJV

Believing that God is without boundaries is essential to living boxed out. He is all knowing, all powerful, and uncontainable. You believe that He loves you, has a plan for you and that completing the work He has for you is part of that plan. You accept your assignments – whenever or however they come – and wholeheartedly believe that you can do anything through Christ who gives you strength. You recognize that there are some walls in your life that have been keeping you from moving forward and you now draw on God's power, presence and Word to tear down those walls. You have taken inventory of your life and have seen that you are, in fact, richly blessed and that God wants to use *you*, as you are. You have laid a solid foundation for your assignment by spending time with God, understanding that while He is the Master Planner, you have a part in the planning process as well. You refuse to stay comfortably contained in your box. You know that God is waiting for you to experience life bigger and better, because He is.

So, this is it. It's time for you to get up and step outside - out of your box and into the world. It's time to put those plans you've developed into motion, in faith. You must have faith in God, His promises, and His ability to help you through this phase of your assignment. Trust that He will be with you now and that the end result of your work will be good. You can't move forward without faith, nor can you please God without it.

> *What does it profit, my brethren, if someone says he has faith but does not have works?*
> *—James 2:14*

However, faith alone is not enough. You have to work out that faith, complementing your trust in God with action. This is not the time to join the League of Armchair Believers, who sit back comfortably, believing with all the faith they can muster up that God will make a way, yet continue to sit on their rears – doing nothing. That's a pretty pathetic and underachieving crowd; don't join it. Nor can we afford to be Church Cheerleaders who jump, clap and praise on Sunday, thinking "Man, that was an awesome message; it's like he was talking to me!" then fizz out by the time Monday rolls around, doing nothing with the word we received. Where is the power in that? There is none! We have to work!

When Jesus performed miracles, He didn't just ask if the people believed they would be healed or delivered,

He also told them to DO something: Go! Stand! Walk! Pick up! They had to work out their faith. Have you ever wondered what would have happened if someone had told Jesus, "Yes Lord! Thank you! I believe in your power and that I'm healed…but I'm just gonna sit here and think about what you've done, because that was some good stuff. I need to let that marinate." Sounds crazy, doesn't it? But that's exactly what we tend to do! We believe from the bench rather than getting up and putting our faith in motion. This is why so many of us remain in our boxes, not at all affecting the world for Christ.

You are now at the juncture where you need to put your plan into play in the real world. This is when you actually <u>do</u> whatever it takes to complete the assignment God has given you. By now, you've already developed your plans, but plans don't construct buildings; crews do. It's people just like you who carry out the tasks as defined in God's plan – by faith and works. Listed below are practical steps you can take to get out of your box, into the world, and about the Father's business.

Work It Out, Step 1: Get organized

Your physical environment has a direct effect on your productivity. Even if your assignment is one that will be performed out in the community, you still need a place to serve as your headquarters – a central place where you work from and keep your files and research. If you have a home office, now is the time to clean it up. Get rid of the clutter, move things out that should be stored elsewhere and clear off your desk or work table. Here are some tips for getting organized:

- If you don't have a designated room in your house that you can use for an office, then use what you have. A desk or table situated away from traffic and noise can be sufficient.

- Round up your research and notes and get them in order. Use binders, file folders, hanging files, or digital files to label and categorize the materials related to the task at hand so that you can easily find them.

- Liven up your work space with wall art, photos, plants and scriptures. All of these can elevate your mood and energy level.

- If possible, invest in a bulletin board or dry erase board for quick-reference and brainstorming. Add a wall calendar so you can quickly visualize timeframes and deadlines.

- If money is an issue, troll the Internet for free stuff or visit a few local thrift stores. Check your garage or basement – you'll be surprised how much of that clutter can be converted into something useful. I'm not ashamed to say that I gave my office a color-themed makeover for less than $30 because of the treasures I found this way.

This first step isn't about winning a home remodeling contest. Decorating and cleaning up are not the end goal – working is. Organizing your workspace is an outward expression of the conscious decision you've made to not only accept your assignment, but to act on it and complete it.

Work It Out, Step 2: Block your work time

In the midst of family, work, church, and friends, you now have to make time for your assignment as well, which seems impossible given the countless demands on your time. We all wish we had more time! The truth is, you don't really need 25 hours in a day, but you can use the 24 you've been given a bit more strategically. You will literally need to *make time*. The time won't be given to you; you'll have to find it, stake claim in it and take it. The following tips can help you find daily or weekly time that you can devote to God's work.

- Lengthen your day by waking up earlier or staying up later, even if you have to train yourself to do so.

- Take a look at your daily and weekly activities and ask yourself which ones can be put on hold or stopped altogether. Are 5 sports per child really necessary?

- Re-read the section on The Wall of Wasted Time and see where you can turn some of those mindless activities into meaningful moments.
- Keep a notebook, journal or tablet with you at all times. In the event you run into a delay or find yourself waiting somewhere with nothing to do, you can convert those minutes from potentially wasted ones into productive ones.
- Once you find time – schedule it. Literally block the time on your calendar as you would a doctor's appointment or interview. Then, honor your appointments with yourself. Use reminders if necessary and communicate with your spouse and kids that you need them to respect this time. (If this works for you, please send me an email on what bribe you offered or what threat you made!).

Your newly-blocked time may be used in-office or to actually get out and do things related to your assignment, such as networking, meeting with a mentor, visiting the library, stopping by a local shelter or senior home, teaching a class, writing code – or whatever activities pertain to your particular assignment. These should be productive hours, focused on carrying out the actions you've already identified in your plan.

Work It Out, Step 3: Schedule your tasks

In order for your blocked time to be productive, you have to do a little more planning (my Type A personality is coming through, huh? Just roll with it!). In order to maximize your productivity, you have to know what you're going to do during your working hours. I have spent many scheduled hours at my desk, time blocked and ready to work, yet accomplished absolutely nothing. There were so many things on my to-do list that I didn't know where to start! A great approach to prevent this from happening is to break down your to-do list into bite sized pieces and schedule them out. Here's how:

- Start with a master task list of all of the action items identified in your plan. It also helps to prioritize this list based on importance of the task – use numbers, color coding, grouping, etc. This will be a living document that changes and grows over time. You can keep this master list electronically or in a notebook, whichever works best for you.

- Next, at the beginning of the week (I do this on Sundays), review your master list for the specific things you want to get done in the coming week. Be realistic – Rome wasn't conquered in a day! Write a star by those items or highlight them with a marker so that those tasks are quickly identifiable (your eyes will focus on those rather than the entire list, which will keep you from feeling overwhelmed).

- Finally, for the items you plan to complete this week, determine which day of the week you will get them done. Pull out your calendar or planner and write out the tasks within the scheduled blocks of time you previously created. If you're using technology instead of paper, use the notes section of your appointment and type in the tasks for that day. This approach gives you a realistic, strategic way of getting work done without being overwhelmed.

If you find that you have more tasks than time, then you may need to reprioritize or spread tasks into the following week. If you need more time, then revisit Step #2 above and see if your time blocks can be expanded. Remember, no excuses. There will be challenges to this well-devised scheme, but it's your response to those challenges that will determine the completion of your assignment. Will you quit in frustration or will you readjust and keep moving forward?

Work It Out, Step 4: Work diligently

God makes it very clear in His word that we are to work with our hands. He said it to Adam in Genesis, and His expectation of us is no different. There are verses throughout the Bible that speak to the importance and necessity of work (provision, sustenance, harvest), as well as the outcome of not working (poverty, destruction). You've come this far by faith, but God will take you even further when you act out that faith. James 2:18 says, "Show me your faith without your works, and I will show you my faith by my works" (NKJV, emphasis mine). Living boxed out – completely committed to using your gifts and talents for God's purposes – doesn't happen without work. You have to activate your gifts - releasing them out into the world so God can use them to rain down showers of blessing on others – and on you. Trust God enough to couple your faith with action. He will make your work fruitful.

By this stage, you've done all the planning and strategizing that you need to do. Now you need to act. Go about completing the tasks that you designated for each of your scheduled blocks of time. Forget about everything else during this time and focus on your tasks for today. Approaching your assignment this way makes it more manageable. Not only that, but being able to check off items on your to-do list gives you a sense of accomplishment. You become emotionally invested in what you're doing. You feel proud of yourself and motivated to move on to the next task, and the next one, and the next. Before you know it, you are deep into the work you've been called to do.

So, if you have been called to write, then write. If you've been called to start a nonprofit, serve on a board of directors or volunteer with one, then get connected and get started. If God wants you to start a business, then take your plan to the next level by ordering business cards and networking. If you've been called to use your crafting skills to make greeting cards for soldiers or seniors in nursing homes, then gather your supplies and create them. Maybe your assignment is to connect with the lady down the street who always smiles but seems lonely. If so, take the next step and invite her over for coffee. If you are led to cook meals for the homeless, then head into the kitchen. If He wants you to develop a website for a school or ministry, then start coding.

I could go on and on, because the possibilities are endless and we each have our own assignments – current and future. Whatever it is that God has placed on your heart to do, this is the time to DO it. Take that plan you've developed and put some action to it. No more sitting around daydreaming. No more talking and thinking. Get up and get to work!

Work It Out, Step 5: Repeat As Needed

You're moving and grooving, actively completing the work of your assignment, and you're doing so in an organized, thought-out manner. The goal now is to keep going. Keep working, keep pressing, keep moving forward. Stay focused on your mission and continue to act on what you've been called to do. This step is meant to help you maintain a state of activity. Newton's First Law of Physics basically states that an object at rest will stay at rest unless an opposing force pulls or pushes on it. Similarly, an object in motion will stay in motion until something pushes or pulls on it. If we think about completing our assignments in terms of this law of physics, then once we get active, we should remain active and moving until something comes along to slow us down, stop us or move us in another direction (you've learned how to deal with the big issues in Chapter 3). We want to keep moving until our assignment is finished, so we need to prepare for those pushes and pulls as best as we can. Step 5 - which is a repeat of Steps 1 through 4 - is how you do that. It's about making adjustments.

As an example, working out your plan will yield output of some type, because work is a productive activity: you put effort in, you get something out. Working out your assignment may produce more things to keep track of − materials, products, files, research, supplies, business cards, etc. As a result, you may need to revisit Step 1 in order to keep your work space organized as you go along. Meeting new people, serving clients, volunteering or other new involvements will mean going back to Step 2 to restructure your blocked time. Scheduling – and rescheduling – your time will be an almost-constant necessity, because things come up and you will need to be flexible enough to make some adjustments as you go along. Your tasks will need to be reshuffled as well. The fact that you are getting things done means, by default, that your to-do list has changed. Some tasks have been completed and others have been added. Repeating Step 3 on a regular basis will ensure that you stay on top of your priorities and operate in Step 4 without being overwhelmed.

This phase of working out your faith is what living boxed out is really all about, because you are actively proclaiming with your life that God can do anything. You become an example of His power, wisdom, love, and grace. You are a living testimony of God using everyday people to do extraordinary things. In fact, the work that you do may not actually feel like work, because it flows from a place of purpose and meaning. It has a value that can't be measured in monetary terms, and it is rewarding in ways that nothing else can match. Working out your faith in alignment with God's plan for your life gives you an inexplicable peace. And the void previously experienced when not acting on your assignment is replaced by joy and fulfillment. Not everything will be perfect, nor will it always be easy, but you know that God is with you. And like a proud parent who beams over a child who has given their best, so will God smile on you as you give of yourself to complete His work.

WORK IT OUT → ACTIONS

1. Create or clean up your workspace.

2. Find one hour per week that you can devote to completing tasks on your Master To-Do List.

3. Schedule that time on your calendar and honor your commitment.

7 - Chase the Horizon

Not that I have already obtained all this, or have already arrived at my goal, but I press on to take hold of that for which Christ Jesus took hold of me.
Philippians 3:12 NIV

The boxed out life is a life of blessing. As you fervently seek to know what God wants you to do and take measures to act on that knowledge, everything changes. When you choose to believe that God is uncontainable, that He gives you power to do His work and then weaves your assignments into His master plan, you will begin to think differently about your own life. You will start to appreciate your value to God – yes, you are valuable to Him! You'll find that you act more decisively - with more intentionality, certainty, and hope - because your path is clear. You know where you're going and what you must do to get there. You'll have a whole new attitude! You will speak differently because you've been communicating with the One who can change the way you talk and your words will be life-giving. You'll respond to circumstances differently, because you recognize that they are only temporary barriers to your mission, and you've been equipped with tools to demolish the walls that get in your way. You'll even begin to look different, because you will have spent time in the presence of God, giving you peace and rest in the deepest part of your soul. "A merry heart makes a cheerful countenance.[5]"

Make no mistake, living boxed out will change your life. You will be blessed in more ways than one – spiritually, physically, and mentally. But this lifestyle really isn't about you at all. Any benefits you may receive out of this process are purely secondary. The ultimate goal is that we honor God and bless others. When your life begins to change because you're walking in your purpose, people will notice. The way you carry yourself in business, ministry or around your neighborhood will raise some eyebrows as people wonder why you seem so content. They will wonder what's going on with you. When they ask the question, be prepared to answer. Tell people why you're happy. Explain to them how you have made a choice to do what matters most in your life – the things that God has gifted you to do. Every question and every curious look presents an opportunity for you to share the source of your hope – God. And just like that, you have impacted a life. Your response becomes a seed planted in that person's heart that someone else can now come along and water. Then God gives the increase. Your simple act of accepting and carrying out your assignment could literally save someone's life. That's why we're here – to be kingdom growers. And that's why we can never quit.

Keep Seeking

Living boxed out isn't a one-and-done deal. It is a lifelong pursuit of the greatness of God being manifested in our lives. After you finish a project, get the business running smoothly, find your place in a ministry position – or whatever your current assignment is – ask God, "what next?" What's next on the Master's agenda for you? When one mission is complete, ask God for clarity on what He would have you to move onto, and look for opportunities to serve others.

The completion of one assignment is not a stopping point in your pursuit; it's just a pause – a moment for you to thank God for what He has already empowered you to accomplish, to pray for His continual blessings on those around you, and to let Him know that you are available for whatever He has next. We have to keep seeking our next assignments, because the harvest is plentiful. There is no shortage of people who need to be reached for Christ, but the laborers, those who are willing to keep working for the Lord, are few. You are one of the few, and your labor of love is needed.

Asking "what next," is how we continue to pursue God's plans for us without letting the grass grow under our feet. The last thing you want to do is complete an assignment and become inactive and complacent once that particular assignment is done. You will need to actively reject the thought that you've done enough and be careful not to settle into a new status quo. Don't feel so accomplished that you sit back down in your box, now with newer, stronger, expanded walls. Living boxed out is a permanent transition, not a temporary placement. For as long as God would have us on this earth, we must seek to do His will, working for Him as long as we're able.

I admire this spiritual work ethic often seen in older, wiser saints – men and women who have been walking with the Lord for years and years, faithfully serving Him for longer than some of us have been alive. Have you noticed how they never quit working? You'll find people in their 70s, 80s or even 90s saying things like, "As long as He puts breath in my body, I'm going to keep on working for the Lord." What an example for all of us to follow!

At the age of 81, after decades of actively serving the Lord in and outside of the church, and 24 years after she had a heart transplant, my grandmother laid in the hospital bed with her body failing. I can't imagine the pain she may have been in or how fatigued she was, but for as long as she could communicate, she asked doctors, nurses, and anyone else who entered her room, "Do you know Jesus as your personal Savior?" She worked for the Lord right on into glory – and so must we.

Keep Pursuing

There will come times in your quest to a boxed out life that you encounter challenges. Not everything will go your way every single time, and this journey won't always be lined with roses. However, don't be afraid of the challenges. Expect them. Remember that you have an enemy, and the moment you decide to do anything that could expand God's kingdom, you become a target for attack. You are basically sending a notice out to the physical and spiritual world that the old, dormant you is gone; the new you has arrived on the scene and is on a mission. The Father, Son, Holy Spirit and the angels in heaven are excited – ready to see you do what was preordained for you to do, and they stand ready to empower and protect you.

> *Be of good cheer, I have overcome the world.*
> *– John 16:33*

But the devil is also ready to work against you. The enemy does not want you to accomplish what you've set out to do, because he doesn't want God to get any glory, and he certainly doesn't want another soul won for God's kingdom. Instead, the devil wants to keep you boxed in - not seeing God for who He is and, consequently, not affecting the world for Him. His futile strategy is to cause fear and to plant lies that cause you to doubt what God said. He wants you to make excuses for why you can't move forward rather than exercising the power of God within you. The devil will attempt to rebuild every wall that you tear down. So his efforts will be to throw any and everything at you in order to distract you or to stop your progress.

However, knowing this upfront is an advantage. Knowing the enemy's strategy enables you to devise a strategy of your own for countering his attacks. What could his tactics look like? Your technology breaks down and you lose all your hard work. You have relationship issues that make it hard for you to focus and cause you to divert your attention elsewhere. Your car breaks down on the way to an important meeting, costing you a new client. Your children become sick or their sibling rivalry moves up to a whole new level. Someone loses a job or is diagnosed with a disease – things that will require a major change, lots of attention and financial resources. You could be presented with an opportunity that seems like a dream come true, but accepting it would mean putting your assignment on the back burner, perhaps indefinitely. Friends or extended family members are going through hard times and you become emotionally and mentally involved in their situations to the point that you just can't deal with anything else.

Or maybe as you work out your assignment, you start to feel that nothing is going as planned and everything seems to be in opposition to your efforts. Your good idea didn't go so well. Someone you were hoping to align with bailed out on you. The funds aren't available. Things seem to be moving very slowly or not at all. You begin to wonder if you're doing the right thing or if you're on the right track. You start to question yourself, and maybe even question God.

In all of these scenarios, as real and as difficult as they may be, understand that things are not always what they seem. Not every situation can be taken at face value. They could be fiery darts thrown at you by the devil to either throw you off track or make you believe you're on the wrong one. That's why we have to put on the whole armor of God[6] – to protect ourselves from the enemy's attacks. When we are geared up with salvation, righteousness, truth, and God's Word, those fiery darts don't stand a chance. Remember Jesus' words, "In the world you will have tribulation; but be of good cheer, I have overcome the world.[7]"

So don't worry! Jesus has already conquered, and He tells us to be of good cheer, because through Him we can overcome as well. Trust in Him and know that the devil can't stop what God has ordained. Memorize scripture and begin to speak God's Word into the challenges you're facing. The Bible is full of life-giving words of power that can be unleashed into any situation, and God's words never fails. Above all, remember the devil has already been

God is bigger than anything that comes against you.

defeated, and we as believers have the authority to remind him of that.

Now, before you go blaming everything on the devil, you have to check yourself as well. Living boxed out - tearing down walls, planning, and acting out your faith - are all hard work, especially when the going gets tough. During those challenging times, you may find yourself resorting to what's comfortable. When you face a roadblock, you may be inclined to turn around rather than go around, because turning around seems easier and less obstructed. You may grow tired and revert to less productive habits, subconsciously rebuilding the Walls of Excuses or Wasted Time.

Let's think of this in terms of getting healthy. If you've ever attempted transitioning to a healthier lifestyle (which is not dieting, but a decision to make a permanent change in the way you eat and exercise), then you know that along with that life-changing decision comes the potential to fall off the wagon. We've all done it at some point. We make a resolution to take better care of ourselves only to lose ground in moments of weakness. Well, falling off the healthy living wagon doesn't usually happen in a crash-and-burn instant. No, it happens one potato chip, one cookie, one missed workout at a time. All it takes is that special occasion where you allow yourself to indulge "just today." It starts by eating just one delicious, calorie-laden dessert because you've worked hard and you "deserve it." Before long, your occasional exceptions have become the new rule and you're right back in the unhealthy box you were oh-so-committed to breaking out of. Beware of the cookie, my friend. Beware of your subconscious telling you that your current task is too challenging and you deserve a break today. Watch out for fear whispering in your ear, coaxing you to believe that the exercising of your faith is just too hard right now and to take a seat in the comfortable chair of complacency. Guard your decision to live boxed out, and commit daily to believing that God is bigger than anything that comes against you - including yourself!

Keep Growing

As you make a conscious daily decision to live boxed out, you will notice that the void that once cast a shadow over your life is diminished or completely gone. The sense of being incomplete and unfulfilled will be replaced by feelings of peace, significance, and hope, because you know that who you are and what you do matter to God, to the people around you, and even to some people you may never meet. This is the true beauty of the boxed out life – that it isn't about you at all. Yes, you as an individual committed to walking in congruence with God's plan can make an impact on the world around you. But what if we all did? What if each of us faced every day with the perspective that God is without boundaries, that He wants to use His people to do great things in His name and that we are part of His plan to display His character to others? What if we all did the things God has placed in our hearts to do? We would change the world!

There are some people in my life whom I personally know are living boxed out. Individually and collectively, they exemplify the boxed out lifestyle. They are very much in tune with their gifts and talents, and everything they do tends to flow from their strengths. They approach each day with a sense of purpose and determination to do the things that matter most. They not only know and accept their assignments from the Lord, but they passionately carry them out – typically more than one at a time – all while looking for even more ways to use what God has placed inside of them to be a blessing to someone else. They're also the hardest working people I know, because they never stop, they never give up, and they never sit down on their talents. These people aren't perfect, but they are at peace, and when I am around them, talk to them or observe them from a distance, I am inspired by their drive to impact their respective communities simply by walking in their gifts each day.

You have the power to change your world, too - one assignment at a time. Since you were fearfully and wonderfully created in the image of God, and because He has given you a predetermined role to play in His plan, you can be confident that the work you do for the Lord is meaningful. Not only that, but your actions and your lifestyle become contagious, affecting everyone around you. The more you seek after God and walk with Him, the more you look like him. The more you look, talk, and act like Him, the more others can see God's character and what it really means to be a Christian. Your "boxed out" life becomes a daily demonstration of the love, power, and grace of God. This is how you change lives and draw others to Christ, which is the ultimate goal.

CHASE THE HORIZON → ACTIONS

1. Within the next 7 days, share with someone why you do what you do (your assignment).

2. Continue the conversation. Engage with like-minded believers on the "Connect" page at **www.LiveBoxedOut.com**.

EPILOGUE

My prayer is that this book inspired you to believe a little bit bigger and trust God a little more. I hope you will trust Him enough to do whatever it is He has placed in your heart to do and worry a little less about the hows, the whens, and the outcomes. My sincere desire is that you realize just how much God loves you and how vast His grace is, and that you discover all that He's placed inside of you. What He has placed in you is meant to flow out of you. The world needs what you have to offer, so I encourage you to start living boxed out. Just begin – today, right where you are.

Please be sure to visit the website built specifically for readers of this book at www.LiveBoxedOut.com. You will find resources and ways to engage with others, as well as the downloadable worksheets and tools referenced throughout this book. You'll also find information about my coaching program and upcoming events. I hope to connect with you online and beyond.

Blessings to you,

robin

REFERENCES

1. Genesis 1:16; 1 Corinthians 15:47; Psalm 147:4
2. Matthew 14:25; Mark 4:39
3. Psalm 103:12
4. Wagner, C. Peter, *Your spiritual gifts can help your church grow.* 1979, Regal Books, Ventura, CA.
5. Proverbs 15:13a NKJV
6. Ephesians 6:10-18
7. John 16:33

ABOUT THE AUTHOR

Robin Smoot has been supporting others in their pursuit of purpose for over 12 years, helping individuals and organizations start and manage their business or ministry, and providing practical solutions to help them get things done more efficiently. Always having an entrepreneurial spirit, Robin pursued her Master's degree to complement her passion, with a promise to God that she would use her gifts and knowledge to edify His Kingdom. This book, her first, is one fulfillment of that vow. Her consulting practice, Boxed Out LLC (BoxedOutLLC.com), is another. Robin enjoys movies, the beach, and anything small business. She is the proud wife of Kevin and mother of three amazing children. She and her family reside in North Carolina.

AN INVITATION

God has a plan and purpose for everyone, which includes eternity with Him for those who have received Jesus in their hearts. If you are not a Christian but desire to be, the Bible says all you have to do is confess, believe, and receive: "That if you confess with your mouth the Lord Jesus and believe in your heart that God has raised Him from the dead, you will be saved." (Romans 10:9). How do you do this? Here's a simple prayer you can say:

Heavenly Father, in Jesus' name I repent of my sins and open my heart to let Jesus come inside of me.
Jesus, You are my Lord and Savior. I believe you died for my sins and you were raised from the dead.
Fill me with your Holy Spirit. Thank You Father for saving me in Jesus' name. Amen.

If you have just prayed these or similar words, Praise God! The angels in heaven are rejoicing over you! And I would love to pray for you as well. Please let me know of your life-changing decision by sending a note to: Connect@LiveBoxedOut.com. Welcome to the family!

www.ingramcontent.com/pod-product-compliance
Lightning Source LLC
Chambersburg PA
CBHW071303040426
42444CB00009B/1847